Inside Animals

Crocodiles

and Other Reptiles

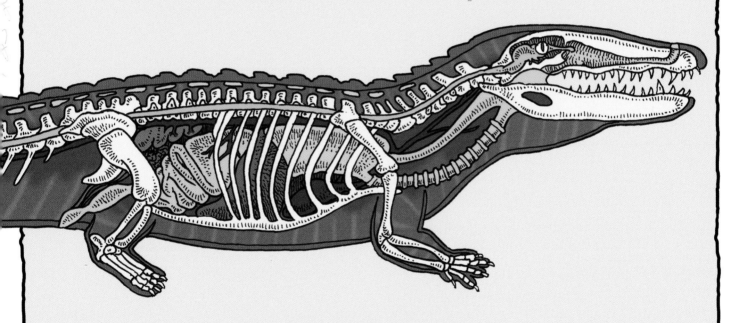

David West

WINDMILL
BOOKS

Published in 2018 by **Windmill Books**,
an imprint of Rosen Publishing
29 East 21st Street, New York, NY 10010

Designed and illustrated *by* David West

CATALOGING-IN-PUBLICATION DATA
Names: West, David.
Title: Crocodiles and other reptiles / David West.
Description: New York : Windmill Books, 2018. | Series: Inside animals | Includes index.
Identifiers: ISBN 9781508194262 (pbk.) | ISBN 9781508193906 (library bound) |
ISBN 9781508194323 (6 pack)
Subjects: LCSH: Crocodiles–Juvenile literature. | Reptiles–Juvenile literature.
Classification: LCC QL644.2 W47 2018 | DDC 597.9–dc23

Manufactured in the United States of America
CPSIA Compliance Information: Batch BW18WM: For Further Information contact Rosen Publishing, New York, New York at 1-800-237-9932

Contents

Lizard

Lizards are the most numerous family of reptiles. They vary in size from a few inches to 10 feet (3 m). The biggest is the Komodo dragon. Like all reptiles, they are covered in scales, and many are brightly colored. Many lizards use their colors to signal to each other.

4

This anole lizard uses its brightly-colored throat pouch, called a dewlap, to signal to other anole lizards. The throat patch is hidden when not signalling, since the bright colors would be seen by **predators**.

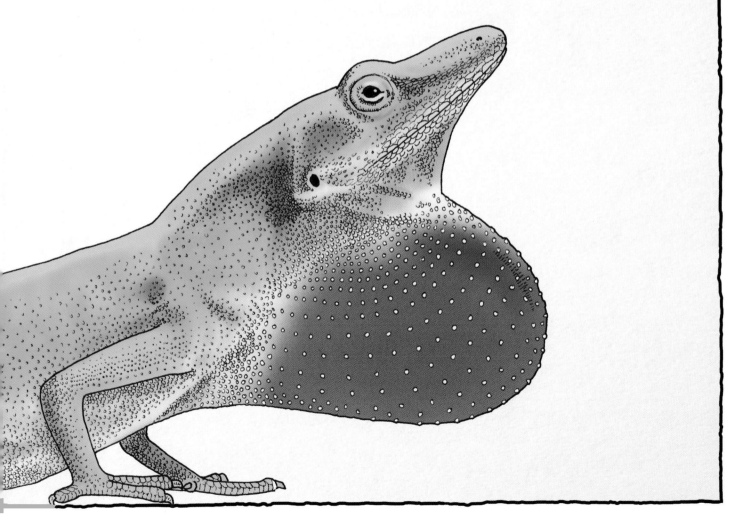

Inside a **Lizard**

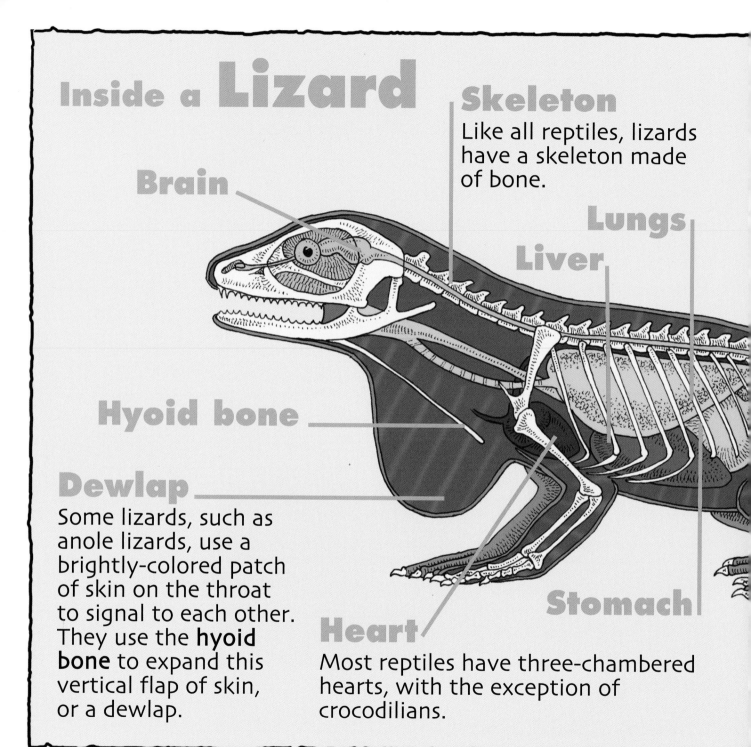

Brain

Skeleton
Like all reptiles, lizards have a skeleton made of bone.

Lungs

Liver

Hyoid bone

Dewlap
Some lizards, such as anole lizards, use a brightly-colored patch of skin on the throat to signal to each other. They use the **hyoid bone** to expand this vertical flap of skin, or a dewlap.

Heart
Most reptiles have three-chambered hearts, with the exception of crocodilians.

Stomach

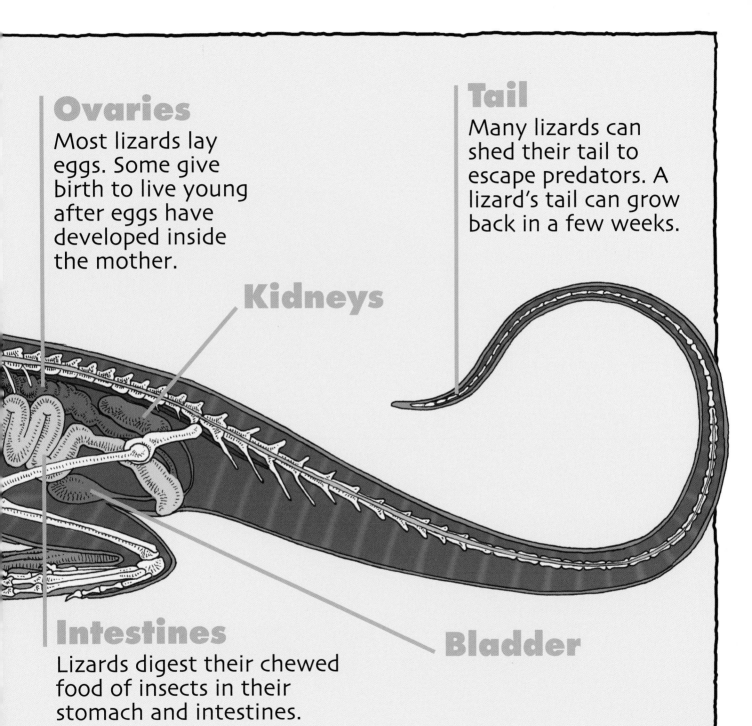

Ovaries

Most lizards lay eggs. Some give birth to live young after eggs have developed inside the mother.

Tail

Many lizards can shed their tail to escape predators. A lizard's tail can grow back in a few weeks.

Kidneys

Intestines

Lizards digest their chewed food of insects in their stomach and intestines.

Bladder

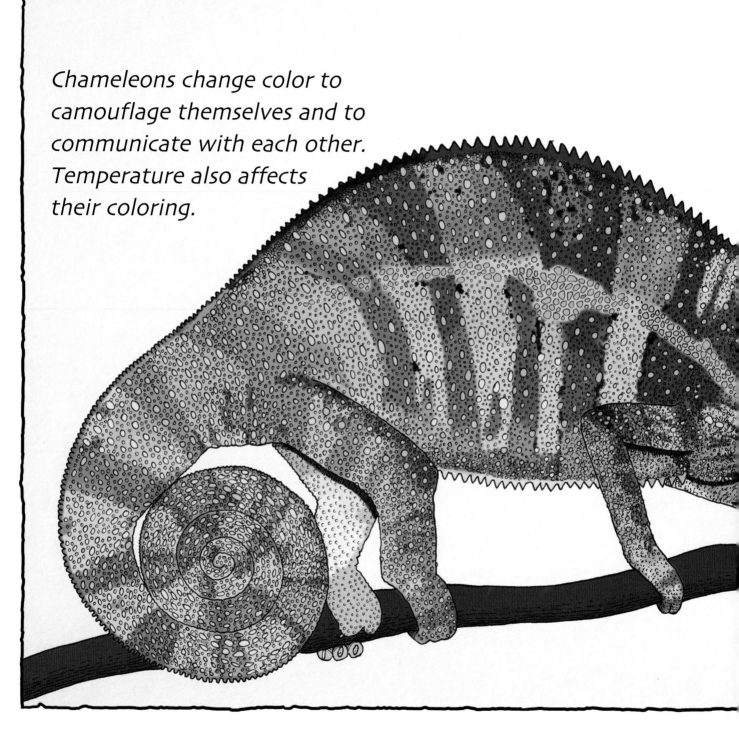

Chameleons change color to camouflage themselves and to communicate with each other. Temperature also affects their coloring.

Chameleon

Chameleons are lizards that can change color to blend into the background. They are excellent climbers. They have special feet that can grip branches, and their tails grip too. Their eyes can look in different directions to spot predators or **prey**. They feed mainly on insects, catching them with their long, sticky tongues.

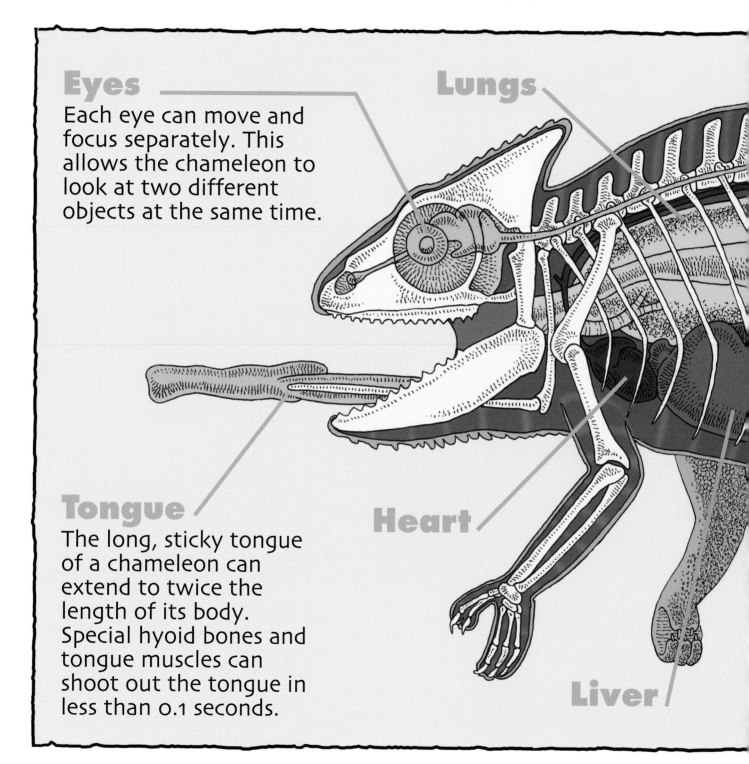

Eyes
Each eye can move and focus separately. This allows the chameleon to look at two different objects at the same time.

Lungs

Tongue
The long, sticky tongue of a chameleon can extend to twice the length of its body. Special hyoid bones and tongue muscles can shoot out the tongue in less than 0.1 seconds.

Heart

Liver

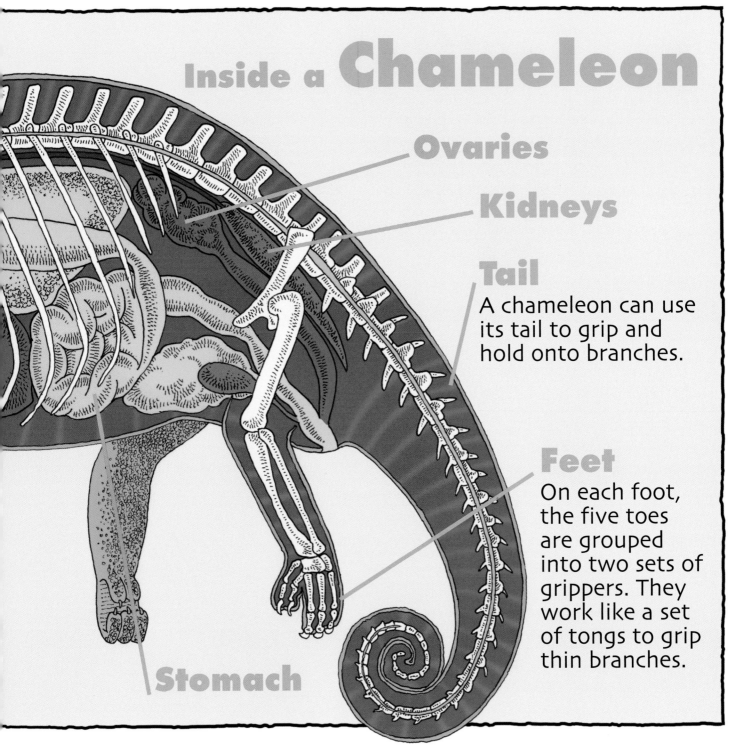

Inside a **Chameleon**

Ovaries

Kidneys

Tail

A chameleon can use its tail to grip and hold onto branches.

Feet

On each foot, the five toes are grouped into two sets of grippers. They work like a set of tongs to grip thin branches.

Stomach

Crocodile

Crocodiles are the largest members of the reptile family. They live in swamps, rivers, and some saltwater environments around the world. They have been around since the age of the dinosaurs and have changed very little since then. They are aggressive hunters and feed on fish, reptiles, **amphibians**, **crustaceans**, **mollusks**, birds, and mammals as large as elephants.

Crocodiles are ambush predators. They wait, concealed underwater, and rush out to grab their prey with surprising speed. Their powerful jaws grip their prey and drag it under the water to drown it.

Inside a **Crocodile**

Armored skin

The outer layer of the thick skin has armored scales, which protect it from predators.

Armored plates

Underneath the outer layer of skin are bony plates called osteoderms. These provide further armor.

Tail muscles

Powerful muscles swing the tail from side to side to power the crocodile through the water.

Skeleton

The crocodile's skeleton has barely changed over the last 200 million years.

Lungs
Crocodiles breathe air, but they can hold their breath underwater for more than an hour

Nose
Its nose holes and eyes are high on its head. This means it can still breathe and see while most of its body lies underwater out of sight.

Kidney

Brain

Throat
Crocodiles have flaps in their throat so that they can eat while submerged without swallowing water.

Liver

Heart
Crocodiles have a flap in their heart that sends extra blood to the stomach to help digest food.

Stomach
The stomach has pebbles in it that help grind up unchewed food.

Turtle

Turtles are reptiles with a special bony shell that protects them from predators. Most turtles can pull their heads into their shell. They all live in water, except for tortoises, which live only on land. There are many types that live their entire lives at sea. They breathe air and lay leathery eggs on land.

*Some turtles, like this terrapin, live in fresh or **brackish** water. They feed on plants and small animals, such as insects, snails, and worms.*

Inside a **Turtle**

Skeleton

The turtle skeleton is divided into two parts, the endoskeleton and the exoskeleton. The internal bones make up the endoskeleton, and the exoskeleton is its shell.

Lungs

Turtles have lungs and must surface to breathe air.

Brain

Head

Some turtles can withdraw their head into the shell for protection.

Heart

Stomach

Liver

This is the largest organ and helps with digestion.

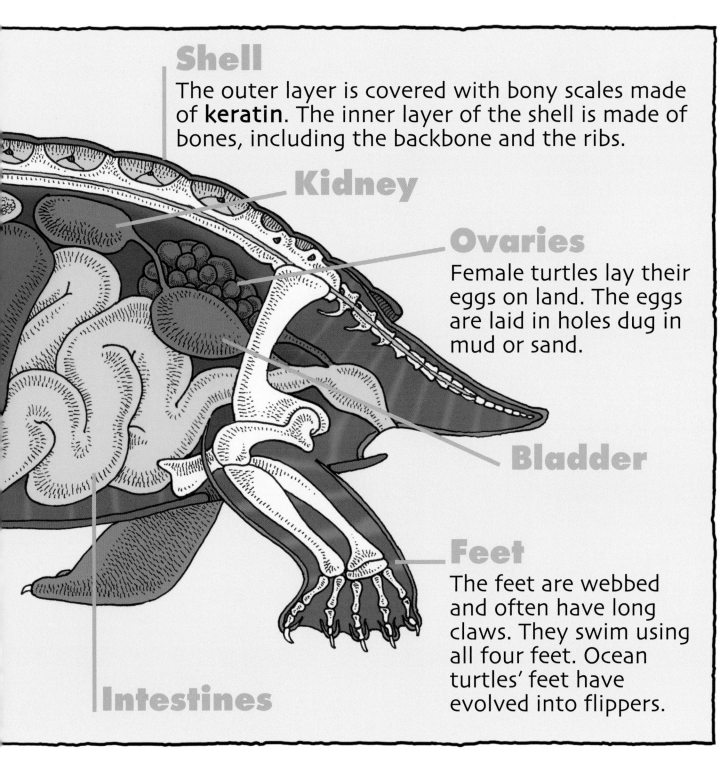

Shell
The outer layer is covered with bony scales made of **keratin**. The inner layer of the shell is made of bones, including the backbone and the ribs.

Kidney

Ovaries
Female turtles lay their eggs on land. The eggs are laid in holes dug in mud or sand.

Bladder

Feet
The feet are webbed and often have long claws. They swim using all four feet. Ocean turtles' feet have evolved into flippers.

Intestines

Snake

Snakes are legless reptiles. Although most live on land, some can be found in the sea. They are cold-blooded like lizards, which means they cannot generate their own body heat. Unlike lizards, they do not have eyelids. Some snakes use poison to kill their prey. They have sharp fangs to inject the poison into the prey. Snakes swallow their prey whole. They have elastic jaws, so they can swallow animals bigger than their heads.

This cobra expands its rib bones to create a hood to warn predators away. It can also squirt venom from its fangs, which can blind its attacker.

21

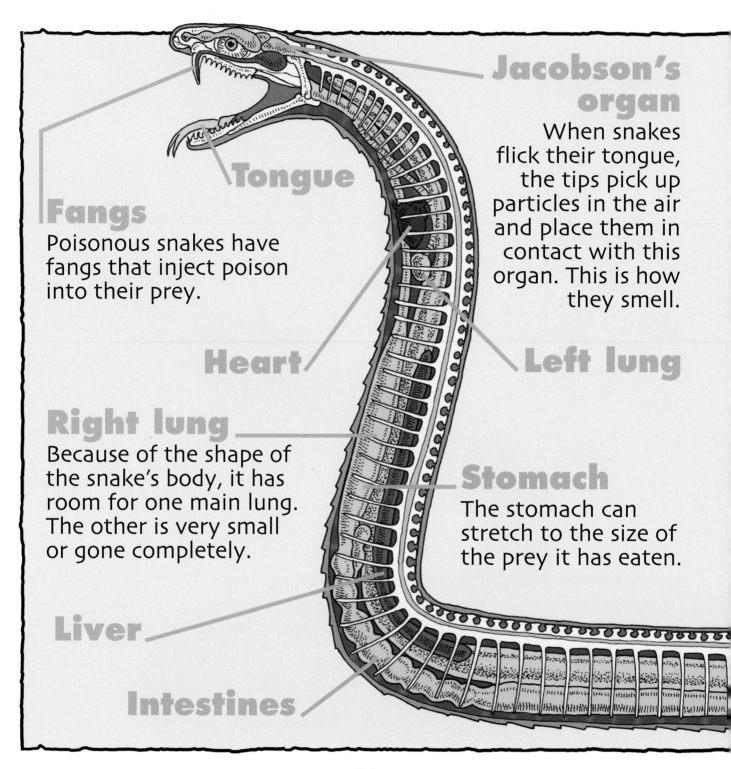

Jacobson's organ
When snakes flick their tongue, the tips pick up particles in the air and place them in contact with this organ. This is how they smell.

Tongue

Fangs
Poisonous snakes have fangs that inject poison into their prey.

Heart

Left lung

Right lung
Because of the shape of the snake's body, it has room for one main lung. The other is very small or gone completely.

Stomach
The stomach can stretch to the size of the prey it has eaten.

Liver

Intestines

Inside a **Snake**

Skin

Like all reptiles' skin, the snake's skin is made up of scales. As it grows, it is shed at certain times. This is called molting.

Ovaries

Most species of snakes lay eggs. The eggs are leathery like most reptiles' eggs.

Skeleton

Snakes can have between 200 and 400 vertebrae in their backbone.

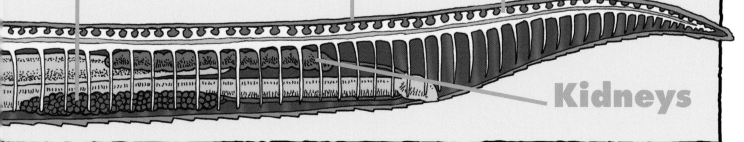

Kidneys

Glossary

amphibian An animal that can breathe in air and water, which includes frogs, toads, newts, and salamanders.

brackish A mixture of river water and seawater.

crustacean A group of mainly water animals that includes crabs, lobsters, and shrimps.

hyoid bone A U-shaped bone in the neck.

keratin A material that makes up the structure of hair, feathers, hooves, claws, and scales.

mollusk A family of animals that includes snails, slugs, mussels, and octopuses.

predator An animal that hunts and eats other animals.

prey An animal that is hunted and eaten by another animal.

Index